The Science of Sleep:
How to Improve Your Sleep Quality and Boost Your Productivity

The Science of Sleep

Disclaimer: The Science of Sleep

The information in the book "The Science of Sleep: How to Improve Your Sleep Quality and Boost Your Productivity" is for general informational purposes only. The author and publisher of this book are not medical professionals, and the content is not intended as a substitute for professional medical advice, diagnosis, or treatment. The strategies, tips, and suggestions outlined in this book are based on general principles of sleep science and productivity research available up to the knowledge cutoff date in September 2021. However, circumstances vary, and what works for one person may not work for another. It is recommended that readers consult with qualified healthcare professionals before making any significant changes to their sleep habits, routines, or lifestyles. The author and publisher do not guarantee any specific results or outcomes from implementing the ideas presented in this book. Sleep and productivity are complex topics influenced by various factors, including but not limited to individual health conditions, medical history, and personal preferences.

The Science of Sleep

Readers are encouraged to use their discretion and judgment when applying the information from this book to their own lives. The author and publisher disclaim any responsibility for any adverse effects or consequences resulting from using or applying the information provided in this book. Furthermore, this book may include references or links to third-party websites, products, or services. Including such references does not imply endorsement or guarantee of the accuracy, quality, or safety of those external resources. Readers should conduct their research and exercise caution when engaging with external content.

"The Science of Sleep: How to Improve Your Sleep Quality and Boost Your Productivity" is intended to provide educational and informative content. Readers should seek advice from qualified healthcare professionals and make informed decisions based on their circumstances before implementing any sleep or productivity routine changes. The author and publisher are not liable for any actions readers take based on the information presented in this book.

Table of Contents

Chapter 1: Introduction

Importance of Sleep and Productivity

In the modern age of constant connectivity and bustling schedules, sleep is often relegated to the backseat of our priorities. Yet, it remains one of the most essential pillars of our well-being. Welcome to "The Science of Sleep: How to Improve Your Sleep Quality and Boost Your Productivity." In this journey through the realm of sleep, we will explore the profound impact that sleep quality can have on our daily lives, focusing specifically on how it intersects with our productivity.

The Crucial Connection

At first glance, sleep and productivity might seem like distant cousins residing in separate realms. However, the reality is quite the opposite. Our sleep patterns, duration, and quality intricately influence our cognitive abilities, emotional resilience, and physical health - all critical determinants of our productivity.

The Science of Sleep

A Holistic Approach

Imagine embarking on a long journey with your body as the vehicle. Just as a car requires fuel, maintenance, and the right conditions to function optimally, so does your body. Sleep is the essential fuel for your body and mind, providing the restoration, repair, and rejuvenation required to meet the challenges of each day.

The Promise of This Book

In "The Science of Sleep," we will dive deep into the science behind sleep - uncovering the mysteries of sleep cycles, the role of circadian rhythms, and the intricate neurological dance that takes place while you slumber. We'll explore the factors that affect your sleep quality, from the environment you sleep into the thoughts that occupy your mind. But this book isn't just about science; it's about practical strategies you can implement to enhance your sleep quality.

Beyond Rest: The Ripple Effect

The Science of Sleep

While sleep is a crucial aspect of our lives, its impact extends far beyond the nighttime hours. We'll uncover how quality sleep can bolster your cognitive abilities, making you more alert, focused, and creative during your waking hours. We'll discuss how sleep plays a pivotal role in emotional regulation, helping you navigate stress and challenges gracefully. Additionally, we'll explore the physical benefits of sleep - from its role in boosting your immune system to its influence on weight management.

Your Personal Sleep Journey

Everyone's relationship with sleep is unique. In the chapters, we'll delve into practical strategies tailored to various lifestyles - whether you're a shift worker battling irregular hours, a student juggling academics and extracurricular activities, or a parent balancing family and work responsibilities. By the end of this book, you'll have a comprehensive understanding of sleep's profound impact and a toolkit of actionable steps to improve your sleep quality and, in turn, enhance your productivity and overall well-being.

The Science of Sleep

As we embark on this enlightening journey through sleep science, remember that every page turned brings you one step closer to unlocking the potential of restful slumber. So, let's begin our exploration of "The Science of Sleep" and discover its transformative power.

Chapter 2: Understanding Sleep

Unveiling the Secrets of Slumber

In our quest to unravel the mysteries of sleep and its impact on productivity, we must first embark on a journey of understanding. Welcome to Chapter 2 of "The Science of Sleep," where we delve into the intricacies of slumber and explore the fascinating world that unfolds when our eyes close.

The Sleep Cycle Symphony

The Science of Sleep

Picture your night of sleep as a carefully orchestrated symphony, with different movements and stages that play a crucial role in your overall well-being. The sleep cycle consists of multiple stages, each characterized by unique brainwave patterns and physiological changes. From the drowsy drifting of Stage 1 to the deep, restorative sleep of Stage 3 and REM (Rapid Eye Movement) sleep, where dreams take center stage, each stage has a specific purpose in the grand performance of sleep.

Circadian Rhythms: The Internal Timekeeper

But the story doesn't end there. Intertwined with the sleep cycle is the concept of circadian rhythms - the body's internal clock that regulates sleep-wake patterns based on a roughly 24-hour cycle. This biological timekeeper is influenced by external factors such as light and darkness, helping us stay synchronized with the natural world. Understanding circadian rhythms is pivotal in optimizing the timing and quality of our sleep.

Behind the Scenes: The Brain's Role

The Science of Sleep

As we drift into the realm of dreams, our brain remains actively engaged in a complex dance of neurotransmitters and neural pathways. The brain's involvement in sleep isn't passive; it's a dynamic process of restoration, memory consolidation, and emotional processing. We'll delve into the fascinating mechanisms that enable the brain to perform these crucial tasks during slumber.

The Many Faces of Sleep: Individual Variability

It's important to note that sleep isn't a one-size-fits-all phenomenon. Each individual's sleep needs and patterns vary, influenced by age, genetics, and overall health. While the average adult might require around 7 to 9 hours of sleep per night, some individuals thrive with slightly less, while others might need more to function optimally. Understanding your unique sleep needs is essential in crafting a sleep strategy tailored to your well-being.

The Road Ahead

The Science of Sleep

As we conclude this chapter, we've taken our first steps into sleep's inner workings. From the intricacies of sleep cycles to the influence of circadian rhythms and the brain's role in the process, we've scratched the surface of this captivating subject. Armed with this knowledge, we're better prepared to explore the factors that can affect sleep quality, impacting our productivity and overall quality of life.

The chapters will explore the environmental, lifestyle, and psychological factors shaping our sleep experiences. By building a solid foundation of understanding, we pave the way for actionable insights that can transform how we approach sleep. So, let's venture forward, ready to uncover the secrets that will lead us to restful nights and more productive days.

Chapter 3: Factors Affecting Sleep Quality

Navigating the Landscape of Rest

As we delve deeper into the realm of sleep, it becomes apparent that achieving restful slumber is influenced by many factors. Welcome to Chapter 3 of "The Science of Sleep," where we explore the dynamic interplay between our sleep quality and our environment, choices, and the thoughts accompanying us into the night.

Setting the Scene: The Sleep Environment

Imagine your sleep environment as the canvas upon which the masterpiece of sleep is painted. Elements such as lighting, noise levels, and room temperature contribute to the overall sleep experience. We'll uncover how a sleep-conducive environment can set the stage for optimal rest, allowing you to drift into slumber without unnecessary disturbances.

The Science of Sleep

In our digital age, screens have become omnipresent, but their glow can have unintended consequences for our sleep. The blue light emitted by phones, tablets, and laptops can interfere with the body's natural production of melatonin, which regulates sleep. We'll explore strategies to manage screen time before bed, ensuring that technology doesn't compromise the quality of your sleep.

The Palate and the Pillow: Diet and Sleep

It might surprise you to learn that what you eat can impact the quality of your sleep. From caffeine's stimulating effects to the soothing powers of certain foods, your dietary choices can influence your sleep cycle. We'll delve into the relationship between diet and sleep, offering insights into foods that can aid or hinder your journey to dreamland.

The Active Rest: Exercise and Sleep

Physical activity has far-reaching benefits for overall health, but its impact on sleep quality is particularly noteworthy. Regular exercise

The Science of Sleep

can help regulate sleep patterns, reduce stress, and enhance the depth of sleep. We'll discuss the optimal timing and types of exercise that can contribute to a better night's rest.

The Mind's Tapestry: Psychological Factors

The mind is a powerful companion during the nighttime hours. Stress, anxiety, and racing thoughts can create a mental storm that disrupts the calm waters of sleep. We'll delve into mindfulness techniques, relaxation exercises, and cognitive strategies that can quiet the mind's chatter, allowing you to ease into restorative slumber.

Charting Your Sleep Terrain

As we navigate the landscape of factors influencing sleep quality, we must recognize that each individual's sleep journey is unique. By assessing your sleep environment, making mindful choices about screen exposure and diet, and adopting strategies to manage psychological factors, you can actively shape the quality of your sleep.

Next Stop: The Impact of Quality Sleep

With a deeper understanding of the factors that can affect your sleep, we're better equipped to move forward on our journey toward enhanced sleep quality and heightened productivity. In the upcoming chapters, we'll explore the manifold benefits of restorative slumber, diving into how quality sleep can elevate your cognitive capacities, emotional well-being, and physical health.

Chapter 4: Benefits of Quality Sleep

Elevating Mind, Body, and Soul

Welcome to Chapter 4 of "The Science of Sleep," where we uncover the incredible array of benefits that quality sleep brings to our lives. Beyond the realm of rest, sleep has transformative power across our cognitive abilities, emotional resilience, and physical vitality.

The Science of Sleep

Cognitive Clarity: Memory and Learning

Imagine your brain as a well-tuned instrument, ready to compose symphonies of thought and creativity. Quality sleep serves as the conductor, orchestrating the consolidation of memories and enhancing learning. We'll explore the science behind these processes and how they contribute to your cognitive prowess.

Focus, Attention, and Creativity

Ever experienced a morning when you wake up brimming with ideas and inspiration? Chances are, your brain enjoyed a restorative night of sleep. We'll delve into how sleep influences your ability to focus, sustain attention, and tap into your creative reservoirs. The synergy between sleep and mental acuity is powerful, shaping your ability to navigate life's challenges.

Emotional Resonance: Mood and Stress

Emotions are the colors that paint the canvas of our lives, and sleep acts as the brush that blends them harmoniously. Adequate sleep is vital for emotional resilience, allowing you to navigate stressors

The Science of Sleep

gracefully and equanimously. We'll discuss the connection between sleep and mood regulation and how the quality of your sleep can determine your emotional landscape.

Physical Restoration: Immune Function and Health

Picture Sleep as the overnight repair shop for your body. While you sleep, your immune system is complex at work, fortifying your defenses against illness. Additionally, sleep plays a role in regulating hormones that impact appetite, metabolism, and weight management. We'll explore how quality sleep contributes to your overall health and vitality.

Balancing Hormones: Sleep and Hormonal Harmony

Within your body, a symphony of hormones orchestrates various bodily functions. Sleep influences the delicate balance of these hormones, affecting everything from stress response to growth and

The Science of Sleep

development. We'll dive into the intricate dance between sleep and

hormones, illuminating how their interplay shapes your well-being.

The Multifaceted Blessing

As we navigate the myriad benefits of quality sleep, it becomes

evident that sleep isn't just a single blessing—it's a multifaceted gift

that enhances every aspect of our lives. From the clarity of thought

to the stability of emotions and the robustness of the body, the

power of sleep reverberates across our existence.

Embracing the Journey Ahead

With each chapter, we're unraveling the tapestry of sleep's influence

on our lives. As we journey deeper into this exploration, armed with

the knowledge of sleep's benefits, we prepare ourselves to tackle the

challenges and implement the strategies. In the upcoming chapters,

we'll equip you with actionable insights to transform your sleep

quality and harness its potential for heightened productivity.

Chapter 5: Strategies for Improving Sleep

Crafting Your Sleep Sanctuary

Welcome to Chapter 5 of "The Science of Sleep," where we roll our sleeves and delve into the practical strategies that can transform your sleep quality. From creating a sleep-conducive environment to establishing a bedtime routine, these actionable steps will pave the way to restful slumber and heightened productivity.

Creating the Ideal Sleep Environment

Imagine your sleep environment as a cocoon of comfort and tranquility, shielded from the chaos of the outside world. We'll discuss optimizing factors such as lighting, noise, and room temperature to craft an oasis of rest. Whether it's blackout curtains to banish light or white noise machines to mask disturbances, these adjustments can make a remarkable difference in your sleep experience.

Mastering the Art of Bedtime Rituals

Bedtime isn't just a moment of transition; it's a sacred ritual that prepares you for the realm of dreams. We'll explore the power of consistent routines before bed, such as reading, gentle stretches, or deep breathing exercises. These rituals signal to your body and mind that it's time to unwind and embrace the soothing embrace of slumber.

Managing Technology for Better Sleep

Managing technology is essential to improving sleep quality in a world dominated by screens and devices. We'll delve into the impact of blue light and ways to minimize its disruption. Establishing technology-free zones before bed and utilizing features like night mode on devices can protect your melatonin production and pave the way for sound sleep.

Relaxation Techniques for Sleep

The Science of Sleep

The path to restful sleep is often paved with relaxation techniques that quiet the mind and relax the body. We'll explore mindfulness exercises, progressive muscle relaxation, and meditation practices that can ease stress and anxiety, allowing you to transition into sleep more easily.

Timing and Consistency: The Sleep Schedule

Imagine your body as a clock, tuned to the rhythm of nature. Consistency in your sleep schedule is vital to sync your internal clock with the external world. We'll discuss the importance of going to bed and waking up simultaneously every day, even on weekends. By honoring your body's natural circadian rhythms, you can enhance the quality of your sleep.

Your Personal Sleep Strategy

As we unravel the practical strategies for improving sleep, remember that this journey is about finding what works best for you. Combining elements from creating a sleep sanctuary, mastering

The Science of Sleep

bedtime rituals, managing technology, and embracing relaxation

techniques, you'll craft a unique sleep strategy tailored to your

needs.

Into the Sleep Haven

Armed with these strategies, you can embark on a transformative

journey into restorative slumber. The tools you've gathered are

more than tactics; they're gateways to a better quality of life, where

sleep becomes a source of rejuvenation and productivity.

In the chapters, we'll tackle specific sleep challenges for different

lifestyles and explore how sleep intersects with productivity in

various spheres of life. As we journey onward, know that each step

brings you closer to unlocking the potential of sleep's transformative

power.

Chapter 6: Sleep Disorders and Solutions

Navigating Challenges for Quality Rest

Welcome to Chapter 6 of "The Science of Sleep," where we confront a topic that affects many: sleep disorders. In this exploration, we'll shed light on common sleep disorders and their impact on sleep quality. We will also delve into medical and non-medical solutions that can help you overcome these challenges and reclaim restful slumber.

Unveiling Common Sleep Disorders

Sleep disorders can cast a shadow over the realm of rest, affecting both quantity and quality of sleep. From insomnia, characterized by difficulty falling or staying asleep, to sleep apnea, a condition marked by pauses in breathing during sleep, these disorders can significantly impact your overall well-being. We'll explore several common sleep disorders, their causes, and symptoms.

The Importance of Diagnosis

Diagnosing sleep disorders often involves collaboration between medical professionals and sleep specialists. If you suspect you're grappling with a sleep disorder, seeking a professional diagnosis is crucial. A comprehensive evaluation can help determine the underlying causes and guide the appropriate action.

Medical Interventions and Treatments

For some sleep disorders, medical interventions and treatments are essential for improvement. We'll discuss approaches such as Continuous Positive Airway Pressure (CPAP) therapy for sleep apnea and medications for insomnia. These interventions are designed to address sleep disorders' specific challenges, enhancing sleep quality and overall well-being.

Exploring Non-Medical Solutions

In addition to medical interventions, non-medical strategies can be pivotal in managing sleep disorders. Lifestyle changes, relaxation techniques, and cognitive-behavioral therapy are the non-medical

The Science of Sleep

solutions we'll delve into. These approaches empower you to take an active role in improving your sleep quality and managing the challenges posed by sleep disorders.

Prevention is often the best course of action regarding sleep disorders. By adopting healthy sleep practices, managing stress, and addressing lifestyle factors, you can reduce the risk of developing sleep disorders in the first place. A proactive approach to sleep hygiene can lay the foundation for long-lasting, restful slumber.

As we navigate the realm of sleep disorders and their solutions, remember that you're not alone on this journey. Whether seeking medical intervention or exploring non-medical strategies, there's a path toward improved sleep quality and overall well-being. By addressing sleep disorders, you're taking a proactive step toward a life of rejuvenation and productivity.

The Science of Sleep

The following chapters will explore the symbiotic relationship

between sleep and productivity in various contexts. By optimizing

your sleep quality, you're positioning yourself to navigate life's

challenges with clarity, creativity, and resilience.

Chapter 7: Sleep and Productivity

Maximizing Your Wakeful Hours

Welcome to Chapter 7 of "The Science of Sleep," where we delve into the fascinating relationship between sleep and productivity. In this exploration, we'll uncover how the quality of your sleep directly influences your work performance, creativity, decision-making, and overall effectiveness.

Cognition Amplified: Sleep and Cognitive Abilities

Imagine your brain as a powerhouse of potential, ready to tackle challenges and seize opportunities. Quality sleep provides the raw materials for this powerhouse, enhancing your cognitive abilities such as memory retention, problem-solving, and critical thinking. We'll explore the science behind these cognitive improvements and how they translate to your productivity.

The Creative Spark: Sleep and Innovation

Creativity is the heartbeat of innovation and thrives in the realm of well-rested minds. We'll discuss how sleep enhances your creative processes, allowing your brain to make novel connections and generate innovative ideas. Whether you're an artist, a writer, or a problem solver, quality sleep can infuse your work with a newfound creative spark.

Productive Decision-Making

From small choices to significant decisions, the quality of your sleep influences your ability to make sound judgments. We'll explore how sleep deprivation can impair your decision-making abilities, leading to impulsivity and poor choices. Conversely, a well-rested mind is better equipped to analyze situations, weigh options, and make decisions that align with your goals.

Time Management and Efficiency

The Science of Sleep

Picture sleep as an investment that yields dividends throughout your waking hours. When you prioritize sleep, you're setting the stage for efficient time management. Rested individuals tend to be more organized, focused, and less prone to procrastination. We'll discuss how quality sleep contributes to effective time utilization and work efficiency.

The Power of Naps

Naps aren't just reserved for children; they can be powerful tools for boosting productivity. A well-timed nap can enhance alertness, improve mood, and sharpen cognitive functions. We'll explore the science of napping, offering insights into the optimal duration and timing of naps to maximize their benefits.

Sleep and Work-Life Balance

The line between work and personal life can blur in the modern world, leading to burnout and decreased productivity. We'll discuss how prioritizing sleep can be pivotal in maintaining a healthy work-

The Science of Sleep

life balance. You create a solid foundation for success in both realms by nurturing your well-being through quality sleep.

As we conclude this chapter, it's clear that the relationship between sleep and productivity is symbiotic. Quality sleep enhances cognitive faculties, fuels creativity, and empowers decision-making. By integrating the strategies for improving sleep into your lifestyle, you're not just enhancing your rest; you're optimizing your wakeful hours for peak productivity.

In the chapters, we'll tailor sleep strategies to various lifestyles and explore how sleep influences productivity in specific contexts. Whether you're a shift worker, a student, or a parent, the principles of sleep's impact on productivity remain universal. So, let's continue this journey, empowered by the knowledge that each night of restful slumber fuels a day of unparalleled productivity.

Chapter 8: Sleep-Boosting Habits for Different Lifestyles

Tailoring Sleep Strategies to Your Life

Welcome to Chapter 8 of "The Science of Sleep," where we embark on a customization journey. In this exploration, we'll navigate the unique sleep challenges faced by different lifestyles - from shift workers to students and parents - and craft sleep strategies that cater to individual needs, ensuring quality slumber and optimal productivity.

The Shift Worker's Guide to Rest

Achieving restful sleep can be challenging for those who navigate irregular hours. We'll discuss strategies to create a sleep routine that adapts to your shifting schedule. From optimizing sleep environments to managing light exposure, you'll discover how to

The Science of Sleep

align your sleep patterns with your work demands, ultimately

improving your well-being and productivity.

Student life is a dynamic blend of academia, social engagements, and

personal growth. Amidst this whirlwind, sleep quality often takes a

backseat. We'll explore strategies to balance your academic pursuits

with a healthy sleep routine. By prioritizing sleep, you'll enhance

your ability to absorb information, manage stress, and maintain

overall health.

For parents, sleep often becomes a rare commodity as the demands

of caregiving take center stage. We'll discuss ways to navigate sleep

challenges while raising children, offering tips for managing sleep

disruptions, establishing bedtime routines, and carving out moments

of rest amidst parental responsibilities. Prioritizing your sleep as a

parent benefits you and your entire family.

Adapting Strategies to Your Lifestyle

While each lifestyle comes with its unique set of challenges, the principles of quality sleep remain constant. We'll guide you through adapting sleep strategies to your specific circumstances, ensuring you can implement actionable steps that suit your needs.

The Unified Power of Sleep and Productivity

Regardless of your lifestyle, the connection between sleep and productivity remains unwavering. By optimizing your sleep quality, you're not just investing in your well-being; you're enhancing your ability to tackle challenges, make informed decisions, and perform at your best.

Charting Your Sleep Odyssey

The Science of Sleep

As we navigate the diverse landscapes of different lifestyles, the underlying truth remains evident: sleep is a fundamental pillar of health and productivity. By tailoring sleep strategies to your circumstances, you're taking a proactive step toward a life where restful slumber fuels your every endeavor.

In the final chapter, we'll reflect on our journey, summarizing the key takeaways and encouraging you to embrace the transformational power of sleep for a life of enhanced well-being and productivity.

Chapter 9: Beyond Sleep - Holistic Well-being

Integrating Health and Productivity

Welcome to Chapter 9 of "The Science of Sleep," where we venture beyond slumber and explore the interconnectedness of sleep, holistic well-being, and productivity. In this exploration, we'll discover how nurturing a balanced lifestyle during your waking hours can enhance the quality of your sleep and elevate your productivity.

The 24-Hour Cycle

Life isn't divided neatly between sleep and wakefulness; it's a continuous, interconnected cycle. The choices you make during your waking hours profoundly impact your sleep quality and overall health. We'll explore how factors such as diet, exercise, and stress management shape your sleep experience.

Nutrition for Vitality

Just as you fuel your car with the right type of gasoline, your body requires proper nourishment for optimal function. We'll delve into the connection between diet and sleep quality, discussing how specific nutrients can promote restful slumber. From foods that contain tryptophan, a precursor to sleep-inducing serotonin, to those rich in magnesium for muscle relaxation, you'll discover how dietary choices can enhance your sleep.

Exercise as a Catalyst

Physical activity isn't just a means to burn calories; it's a catalyst for improved sleep quality. Regular exercise can help regulate circadian rhythms, alleviate stress, and enhance the depth of sleep. We'll explore how incorporating movement into your routine can lead to more restful nights and energized days.

Stress Management and Sleep

The Science of Sleep

Stress is inevitable, but its impact on sleep can be mitigated through effective stress management techniques. We'll discuss mindfulness practices, meditation, and relaxation exercises that can help you navigate stressors resiliently, ensuring they don't disrupt your sleep quality.

Holistic Approach to Well-being

Quality sleep isn't an isolated endeavor; it's part of a more extensive journey toward holistic well-being. By nurturing a balanced lifestyle encompassing physical, mental, and emotional health, you create a fertile ground for restful slumber and heightened productivity. Remember that sleep is a reflection of your overall state of well-being.

A Flourishing Life

As we approach the conclusion of this exploration, consider the life you're crafting—one where sleep isn't a mere necessity but a deliberate choice to nurture your body, mind, and soul. By

The Science of Sleep

embracing a holistic approach to well-being, you're aligning yourself with the rhythms of nature and positioning yourself for a life that flourishes in both rest and activity.

In the final chapters, we'll summarize the key takeaways from this journey and empower you to embark on a path where sleep and productivity intersect harmoniously. You're setting the stage for a life of purpose, joy, and meaningful accomplishments by cultivating a lifestyle that values rest and vitality.

Chapter 10: Embracing the Sleep-Productivity Nexus

As we reach the final chapter of "The Science of Sleep," reflecting on our enlightening journey together is fitting. We've explored the intricate world of sleep, uncovering its profound influence on our cognitive abilities, emotional well-being, and physical health. From creating sleep sanctuaries to mastering bedtime rituals, we've armed ourselves with strategies to transform the quality of our rest.

The Power of Transformation

Throughout this book, we've witnessed the transformational power of sleep. We've learned that sleep isn't a mere pause button in our lives; it's a dynamic process that repairs, rejuvenates, and equips us for the challenges ahead. By prioritizing sleep, we've set a chain reaction that cascades into heightened productivity, improved decision-making, and overall well-being.

A CALL TO ACTION

The Science of Sleep

As you close this book, remember that the journey of sleep optimization doesn't end here. It's an ongoing commitment to self-care and holistic well-being. The knowledge you've gained is a compass guiding you toward restful nights and more productive days. But knowledge alone isn't enough; your actions will ultimately shape your sleep quality and, consequently, your quality of life.

Your Sleep Odyssey

Consider this book as the first step of your sleep odyssey. Armed with insights and strategies, you're now equipped to navigate the complexities of sleep in an increasingly fast-paced world. Whether you're a shift worker, a student, a parent, or seeking better sleep and heightened productivity, the principles outlined here can be tailored to your needs.

The Ripple Effect

As you embark on this journey, remember that optimizing your sleep quality isn't just a solitary endeavor; it has a ripple effect. Your

The Science of Sleep

enhanced well-being and productivity resonate throughout your life - from personal relationships to professional accomplishments. By embracing the symbiotic relationship between sleep and productivity, you're shaping a future where each day is lived to its fullest potential.

Dream Big, Sleep Well

In a world that celebrates hustle and bustle, it's easy to overlook the importance of rest. But now, armed with the knowledge of sleep's transformative power, you can craft a life that embraces productivity and rejuvenation. So, dream big, aspire to great heights, and remember that quality sleep is the foundation upon which your aspirations can flourish.

Thank you for joining me on this journey through "The Science of Sleep." As you step back into your wakeful hours, may you carry the wisdom of restful slumber and the promise of a more productive, fulfilling life.